Copper and Other Precious Metals

Poems from the Core

Elaine McMilian

Reader Comments

"Elaine McMilian's poems capture joy and grief, beauty, and pain. They wrestle with loss and betrayal, celebrate truths large and small, and explore pathways toward acceptance of life's challenges. *Copper and Other Precious Metals* is full of wisdom, courage, determination…and a wry sense of humor."

— Sharon Blevins, scholar, writer, citizen

"Elaine's poetic storytelling is deeply affecting in its heartfelt disposition and steadfast in its delivery. Her writing maintains unwavering realism, but also unquestionably inspires hope. Elaine's writing testifies that there cannot be joy without despair and vice versa."

— Eric Vajentic, philosopher, writer, *Cosmic Contortions* at ericvajentic.substack.com

"Using courage and memory as its needle and thread, McMilian's work sews together the story of a life through grief, acceptance, and reflection. Filled with deep internality and brave, accurate language, *Copper and Other Precious Metals* brings the reader face to face with the emotional realities of loss, heartbreak, and pain, but also with the acceptance and recognition of the same — which is laid down in this book with grace and majesty. *Copper* is hewn from the heart of the poet, and infused with a voice ringing with clarity, sincerity, and love."

— Dana Huffer, scholar, writer, *Sentinel of Anecdotes* at danahuffer.substack.com

This book is for my living loves:

Gaylon
Suzette, Andrew, Isaac, Judah, Joseph,
Zac, Andrea, Josie, Hazel, Rosslyn
Blake

And my missing loves:

Ben, Donald, Ruth, Mark, Brian, Tom

Kindness is everything.

Preface

Whether I'm writing poems, stories, or songs, I choose memoir to connect with others also going through the hardships of life. I believe that how we treat each other is our purpose for living. Writing about what we experience is not only therapeutic, it helps us see how we've survived, and even better, thrived. As for me, I'm still figuring it out as I go and assume everyone else is, too.

I know a lot about loss and grief. Between the years of 1998-2008, I lost two brothers, both parents, and my beloved son, Ben. During that time my surviving brother went to prison for life (a whole other story). Then a four-year respite until my partner Tom died suddenly from a heart attack.

People say things to me like: "It's the worst thing that can happen to a parent," or, "I don't think I could survive that," or, "How do you keep going after what you've been through?"

I agree that losing a child — whatever their age — is absolutely the worst thing that can happen to a parent. Part of me died with him. Going through these losses has changed my view of death, which I no longer fear, and of our precious time on earth. In spite of grief, I'm very much alive and happy. Living fully with love and joy, engaged and active, is how I choose to honor my loved ones and myself. We can carry on.

Death has a way of affecting everything. Losing my son was the most profound experience of my life. Some of the poems in this book are about heartache, loss, and grief. But I also write about birth, family, falling in love, making mistakes, friendship, sleep, and nature. I live, love, and create because despite it all, I am hopeful.

Table of Contents

Footprints

I stepped into footprints carved
centuries ago, along elevated pathways
of the New Mexico mesa, a sign
of survival that defied hardship.

Foremothers of every people
carried wisdom in handwoven baskets
or clay pots, lessons about nature,
perseverance, and fortitude.

A mountain breeze lifts ancient songs
across wide oceans and vast prairies.

My ears tune to the singing wind,
eager to know their secrets.

A Dream of Something Better

My parents were young, once.

Curious and ambitious,
a smalltown boy folded big ideas
into his one good shirt and
took the train to the nearest city.

Timid and unsure, a teenage girl
wearing bottle cap glasses
and a homemade dress
walked to her first job at JCPenney.

Noticing the new salesclerk
with dreamy chocolate eyes and
soda pop smile, she applied
new pink bubblegum lipstick.

"Wanna see my new car?" he flirted.
"Sure!" she gushed, imagining a future.

Two kids with nothing but hope,
their pasts evaporating in the wake
of exhaust fumes and speeding tires.

Buttons

Sprawled on Mom's bed,
I searched for gleaming gems,
pearls, or matching sets
in the red-and-white striped
button box.

Sewing machine whirred
a hypnotic rhythm
as she made an Easter dress
or tiny stylish clothes for my
red-bubble-haired Barbie.

Now mine, buttons fall like
pirate's treasure through
my pin pricked fingers,
shiny mementos of happy times.

The Confession

Angry voices sliced through midnight's quiet,
my young ears on high alert.

"How long?" hissed my mother.
"Three years," came his reply.

I heard it all: the crying, the anger, the pain.

Next morning, called downstairs to the
dining room table, my father told us
he was leaving.

Rented an apartment I never visited,
married a woman I never met.

He brought her to my brother's junior high
basketball game. Real skinny, black beehive
hair, vampire red lips.

I glared at her.
She looked like a witch.

Seventh Son

This little girl thought you were everything.

In a shoe box of faded photos,
I found your freckled, farm boy face,
grinning teeth not yet settled.

High school picture boasts
a winsome smile, thick hair
waving like a movie star.

Young man's professional
portrait, your handsome face now
poised, confident.

Before the booze took over.

I'm not angry anymore, but I'm curious.

Johnny Rivers sang:

"Did you know you had special powers,
To heal the sick and raise the dead?
Predict the rain?
Make the girls talk outta their heads?
The seventh son, you were the one."

Youngest of seven boys, you were the seventh son.
If only you'd known about your special powers.

To me, you were the one.

Moon Landing, 1969

Where were you when astronauts landed on the moon? That summer of 1969, I was at church camp, attending the evening service in the tabernacle, with televisions on the stage instead of preachers. But all I could see was my crush with his arm around another girl. A school classmate, I was jealous of everything about her. She was pretty, popular, and smart. They sat in the back row of wooden seats to avoid eyes less observant than mine.

Six years later I married that boy…and eventually divorced him. However, the pretty girl became one of my best friends. A deeply caring person, she's engaged with the world and of service to people. Plus, she laughs at my jokes. I treasure our lifelong friendship and the memories we share, including those of my former crush.

Humans landed on the moon, and history was made. Sometimes we don't really know what we're looking at.

Limbo

Pale skin, white sheets,
our beloved matriarch
lies suspended in limbo,
above mortals, below gods.

We barely breathe,
praying for her release…
and ours.

Ascending

Undeterred
by cancer's death
sentence, he chose to
live fully while oxygen
still flowed to his weakening
heart. The doctor said, "It's time
to call hospice." Back at home, refusing
help, he sat down on the bottom step and
pulled himself up the stairs to the kitchen,

                              victorious.

Off Balance

Grief rocks the world off balance.

Fingers grab blindly at stability,
crumbling at every touch.

Time crawls slowly through
the dark hole of infinite night.

Daylight pries at my eyes
like a toddler staring me awake…

Persistent, forceful, demanding.

Lifeblood

Wisps of copper newborn hair,
hearts of mother and child beat
in synchronized rhythm.

Lifeblood pulses strongly through our veins.

Bright-eyed boy grows into
an eager young man, his goodness
glowing like a star in the dark.

Lifeblood pulses strongly in his veins,
until it doesn't.

Who knows our unique life cycle?
Birth, and death.

Sparks float into the ether.

I search the vast expanse of night's sky,
my child a swirling copper thread
throughout the universe.

Home Birth

We chose to do a home birth, just the two of us.
Hours of reading, classes, and exercise led up to this
highly anticipated event. When my water broke it was
time to get into position, so we arranged a nest made
from newspapers and plastic trash bags, played
Scrabble, and timed contractions, aware that each
increased intensity brought you closer to emergence.
One final push propelled you from my womb into
your father's waiting hands, your slippery body
covered in natural protective cream. And then, you
unfolded like the most beautiful flower, blooming
before our eyes like pure love.

Calla Lilies

Alabaster headstones bloom
across green hills,
calla lilies in heaven's garden.

Soldiers who came home
with medals
or cancer
from chemical warfare,

identical flowers
except for the one that is
my son.

The Fox

Dancing flame against
rows of silent stones,
a red fox sets the
tombstone garden ablaze.

Stopping once,
where earth absorbed
my tears.

A sign from my son?
Hair at birth bright as
a new copper penny.

Surprised

On a morning walk, snow surprises me
as gauze doilies blanket my hair.

Sudden tears melt snowflakes.
Today is my son's birthday.

Instinctively, my head tilts up.
Lacy ice delights my ready tongue.

Images flash like an old-time movie,
his ready grin an invitation
for mischief or enlightenment.

At that moment, remembering,
I'm thankful.

Wounded

Tender hearts and delicate psyches
make for vulnerable targets
on life's rocky terrain.

Barriers in place, eyes dart,
senses alert. Something painful
might be coming this way.

Wounds roughly held together
like old, ripped jeans.

Are we ever wholly healed?

Forever changed,
battle scar medals decorate
my weathered skin.

Pyromania

Fireflies illuminate night's veil,
expose our simmering intentions.

Breezes ignite ready sparks;
rumors whisper behind lace curtains.

Dancing on white-hot embers,
pretend you don't feel it.

One smoldering look,
we're up in flames.

Tarnished

I thought I saw your car…
every silver car might be yours.

In fairy tales, shining armor
gleams self-assurance.

In real life, silver tarnishes
from neglect.

Today, I flinched.

Tomorrow, I'll look away.

Soon, I won't care.

New Love

First time together,
She, love starved and timid,
He, kind and gentle.

Ecstasy turns to tears
for the neglected child,
broken heart,
grieving mother.

She cries for this new lover,
who doesn't know
what he's in for.

Sleeping, or Not

Sleeping,
not me, but you.

Discordant chimes compose
night's soundtrack.

A foot escapes tangled linen.

Soft, rhythmic breathing fuels
dreams I can only imagine.

Watching you,
I doubt I'll sleep tonight.

Self-esteem

I found my self-esteem,
discarded like lace panties
under the bed.

Tenderly, I slip it back on
over battered ego and wizened
brow, ready to forgive.

Dead Space

At the end of the bar,
a tipsy regular chugs cheap beer,
laughs loudly at his own jokes,
while a raccoon-eyed barmaid
feigns interest for tips.

Across the dim, stale room,
marooned lips weave sad stories
through minor guitar chords.

Music dissipates into the dead space
between them.

Playtime

A tiny maestro, she directs me
down to the floor to play.

Barbies pulled from a chaos
of plastic bodies and rainbow hair,
we dig for accessories hidden
in piles of miniature platform shoes.

She bakes treats for our tea party
in a pint-sized stove, placing
plastic cookies on pink plates.

"Eat like this, Grandma!" she instructs,
smacking sugar-coated lips.

Both of us weary, she finds a favorite
book, then settles into a child's
vintage rocking chair, her name
painted across the top by my hand.

Holding Hands

A grandma's habit, I reached
for his hand, even though he's ten
and can cross the street on his own.

"Oh, sorry!" I sputtered,
"I know you don't need to hold my hand."

"No, but you do," he countered,
holding on tight.

Boots

I still see him waiting outside
the Thai restaurant, legs crossed,
blue eyes reflecting the April sky.
After dinner, a goodbye kiss
that says Hello.

Days drift by with writing,
music, and conversation.
We survive on pennies and love.

One day his father died. "We're
not poor anymore," he tells me.

Spying the boots in a store window,
he insists I try them on, easing my feet
into the buttery shaft of the black leather
Lucchese 1883 Handcrafted Cowboy Boots
with a Snip Toe.

They feel like heaven.

Six weeks later, I wore my fancy
boots with a sale-rack black dress
to his unexpected funeral.

Dazed, the boots carried me
behind the simple pine casket.

Now, when I wear my black leather
Lucchese 1883 Handcrafted Cowboy Boots
with a Snip Toe,
I remember my generous lost love,
who wanted only the best for me.

Flags

His family received the Army's honorary flag
and wondered how it ended like this.

A streetwise Phillie boy, he outran gangs
and beat up boarding school bullies,
protector of the vulnerable except for himself.
A West Point grad and Army Ranger,
he deflected bullets and blew up ships,
sometimes awake for days.

Upon his return, the weary soldier faced
war at home, marriage an inevitable casualty.
Lured by a fresh start to an English pub,
he washed bed linens and fried fish while
deflecting fists of an alcoholic second wife.

Tragic news of a car accident strained
his weakening heart. He cried out,
"How could you take my son?"

Back in the U.S., jobs hid like fugitives,
PTSD lurked in every crowd. Vets held
cardboard signs at intersections.

"I considered that," he confided.

Admirers often remarked,
"He's the smartest man in every room."
"He's the kindest man I've ever known."

Until that day, on a simple walk to get
coffee, his exhausted heart stopped.

A final white flag, surrendered.

*Ciggies**

If I had a cigarette, I'd smoke it. I've only smoked two cigarettes in my life, and I hate them, but if I had one here and now, I'd smoke it all the way down. "Ciggies," he called them. He was considerate of my dislike and smoked only outside, downstairs by the lobby. But if I had a ciggie right now, I'd hold it up in the air like a glass of bubbly, and say to no one, "For you, my love."

I'm thinking of his loft in downtown Kansas City at 17th & Walnut. It had one window set into a brick wall which looked out onto the city street, the world going on around us. What did we need a window for?

After our French-pressed morning coffee, we'd lounge on the oversized orange sectional couch, feet up on the matching footstool, laptops or newspapers or journals in hand. Sometimes we listened to Billy Strayhorn's kaleidoscope of music; other times preferring the sound of sleek red Ferrari's, old beat-up Hondas, and scooters-for-rent whisking by outside, tires spitting last night's rain from puddles on the street.

Later, we'd go for a walk through the grid of city blocks, climbing west to view the progress of the new performance hall designed by Moshe Safdie. He loved telling the story of the time they met. After picking up groceries at Coscentino's Market, after bumping into each other as we cooked in the tiny kitchen, after relaxing on the big couch with glasses of wine, we'd finish the day by falling into bed, sharing our life stories long into the night.

The smell of cigarettes always brings it back to me.

Inspired by the poem "Sunday Night" by Raymond Carver, a WWKC prompt.

Turning

Those first weeks in our downtown loft,
I couldn't find my way home.

One-way streets led the wrong direction.
At each corner, tall stone sentries
ignored my distress.

Years later, I visited our former place,
standing on the sidewalk where he died
from a heart attack.

Grounded, I know where I am,
and where I'm going.

The Psychic

He didn't tell me about the chest pains,
thought he could walk it off.

Lost in the emptiness of sudden death,
I went to a psychic.

"You must be so angry," she began,
"It's okay to be angry."

"Someone will ask you to lunch,
someone respectful and waiting.

You'll get a job offer.

Everything will be fine,
including a miracle," she proclaimed.

I accepted both offers, the man and the job.

Forgiveness is a miracle.
Love is a miracle.
Life is a miracle.
Resiliency is a miracle.

Joy Amidst Grief

As I walked down the hall, moving from class to class, every teacher reached out to hug me. Preschool students handed me colorful cards and posters.

A week before, the world stopped turning…except it didn't. It swirled around me, disorienting. Immobile with grief, I barely breathed. My partner of two-and-a-half years had just died of a sudden heart attack.

Re-entering daily life at my new job as a music teacher, the day began with singing children gathered around me, tempering grief with joy.

What If?

What if a person dies and love doesn't,

but instead lives on
in dreams,
in longing,
in questions?

Two years seems barely a beginning.
A future unexplored, potential undefined,
a life together cut short.

Would we have stayed in that loft?
Created an art collective in Midtown?
Would we have been happy?

"There's no 'there' there," he used to say,
looking for substance where there was none.

No longer there,
I'm left with what ifs.

Love and Grief

Once grief arrives it never leaves,
burrowed in the space
of whoever left.

Love is the mother of grief.

Together, love and grief
nurture sorrow into compassion.

Perennials

Slumbering plants splash awake
by sun rays and raindrops.

Posies, butterflies, and hummingbirds
spill across Earth's canvas like
Pollock's spattered paint.

Each masterpiece promises to be
more beautiful than the last.

The Mountain King

High stepping through a wall
of statuesque pines, the moose
lumbers toward the salt lick
outside of our mountain cabin.

A mile-wide "crown of courage"
tops his impressive muscular frame.
We city folk revel in this
rare sighting of forest royalty.

Finished with his morning treat,
and our astonished stares,
the mountain king disappears
into the lush Colorado forest.

Ode to Resting

Trees shed their leaves to prepare for Winter's sleep,
landing like a crazy quilt on life that lies beneath.
Tiny creatures, roots, and bulbs safely hide below.
Quietly, they wait until it's time to sprout and grow.

What lessons can be learned from the cycle
   of plant life?
Patience? Purpose? Trust things will turn out right?
Bursts of creativity, then we allow ourselves to rest.
Artists, like nature, need quiet time to be their best.

Summer wilts into Fall as swirling winds disrobe
   the trees.
Good things will bloom again if we choose to believe.
Spring nurtures a rebirth, offers hope, and I, for one,
favor the idea that resting helps me get things done.

Welcome

The house was bigger than I expected, although I didn't know much about this man.

Introduced by a mutual friend, we were both performing musicians, he in the classical genre, and me, the local rock circuit. The tutoring clinic where I worked needed teachers, and his background included helping people learn to read. At our first lunch we discussed the schwa and Bartok, which we took as a very good sign.

We both lost partners to illness. He renovated his home. I started dating again. We found each other at the exact right time.

As I walked up the steps, I could see his beaming face through the front door window. His first words to me: "You're here."

Ten years later, I'm still here.

Hand Sewn Quilt

Each time I started over, the box
labeled "Quilt" traveled with me,
a reminder of my unsettled life.

Inside, pastel patterned fabric, some
pinned with handwritten notes from
my grandma's nimble hand.

Each block unique, memories return
of how to match seams and sew
intricate designs on borders. Just like
life, some techniques took practice,
tiny stitches ripped out until I got it right.

Finally, the squares unite into
a finished work of art.

My hand sewn quilt, an homage to
my mentors, an heirloom for
my progeny, a comfort to myself.

Elusive

Reclined on a magic carpet,
gently drifting like lapping waves
on soft sand,

clouds soften the watchful moon
as stars guide ships afloat
in sky and sea.

Glow of a distant lighthouse
fades upon approach…

sleep remains elusive.

Saving Myself

Sensing danger,
I stepped out of the dream
just in time
to save myself
from impending doom…

a skill I wish for when I'm awake.

Sleep Writing

In that hazy consciousness
between sleep and dreams,
random ideas connect,
hinting at sentences and themes.

Eyes twitch until blinked awake.

Phone texts become temporary memos,
holding onto the muse until morning.

No Joy at Christmas

Countless souls wait for rescue,
sleep on tarps at borders,
stuck at sea, traumatized by war,
hungry, poor, oppressed.

Violence rampant across the ocean
and here, too close to home.

Holiday lights explode in bold colors,
blaring America's wealth and freedom,
visible from outer space.

Enraged, confused,
I can't find joy in this world.

No Santa or God can save us.

To My Living Loves

Reasons to write about my living loves
surface less often than for those I've lost.

Grief hides like an infection in my scars,
inflames at the smallest reminder.

Happiness in daily life flows like a
gentle breeze, my loves and I sharing
the same air.

We travel together, taking walks,
wilderness hikes, or a trip to Santa Fe.

Inside our cozy homes, we eat ice cream,
listen to Bartok and Pink Floyd,
or debate philosophy while playing games.

To my loves that I can touch, hear,
and see, who nurture my heart…

because of you, I live.

What I Know, Now

I knew everything, once,
forging ahead with innocent chutzpah
while scavenging truth along the way.

No one tells you these things:

No one knows how to be a parent…
including your own.
No one wants to admit their worst mistakes.
Beliefs, systems, and rules might protect you,
but can also control you.
No one wants you to know that it's all made up.
Much of what I thought I knew were lies.

I knew everything, once, when I was young,
before I knew anything at all.

Here's what I know now:

Dive into the deep.
Make mistakes; it's the only way to learn.
Accept uncertainty.
Make up your own mind.
Determine your core values and live by them.

If someone truly loves you, they will not
intentionally hurt you.

If someone hurts you, leave.

It's possible to fall in love again, and again.

But the most important thing to know is this:

Be compassionate, love with grace.

Acknowledgments

I'm deeply thankful for my patient and insightful
Beta Readers: Sharon Blevins, Dana Huffer, and
Eric Vajentic. Your willingness to spend valuable
time reading my manuscript and providing thoughtful
feedback is humbling, and a true gift.

For the past eight years, my Writing Posse (Sarah
Baum, Sharon Blevins, Bibie Chronwall, Maureen
Huffer, LaDene Morton, and honorary member
Patrick Dobson), has served as eyes and ears to my
dreams, scribblings, and journey toward creating this
book of poetry. Your support and friendship mean so
much to me, and I'm thankful for each one of you.

Writing Workshop KC, led by the inimitable Frances
Story, has become my home, my safe place, and my
people. I've told Frances numerous times that the
experience she creates there is magical…because
she is magical. Each one of you amazes me every
time we meet, online or in person, and provided the
motivation I needed to write and produce a complete
work of poetry. I'm thankful to you all, and
especially John Raux, my hero, who stepped in at the
final hour to help me get it done.

My dear friends, old and new, are a blessing in my life. Too many to name, I love you.

My husband, Gaylon, provides the foundation for my creative pursuits. His wisdom keeps me grounded, and his love allows me the freedom to follow my dreams. I love you and thank you with all my heart.

To my son, Zac; daughters-in-law, Andrea and Suzette; and grandchildren, Andrew, Isaac, Judah, Jo, Josie, Hazel, and Rossi: I am infinitely thankful for your unconditional love and constant inspiration. I learn from each of you every time we're together. My life's greatest joy, everything I do is because of my love for you.

About the Author

Elaine McMilian wrote her first poem in junior high school, and whether it's poetry, songs, or essays, she's been a committed writer since. After graduating from the University of Missouri-Kansas City with a Creative Writing degree, she worked as a musician in genres as diverse as folk, alternative, classic rock, jazz standards, and punk. In more recent years, she's shifted toward writing poetry and essays, showcasing her works in her original blog, *And Something Else*, and her current online site, *And Something More.*

Elaine lives contentedly in Kansas City, Missouri, with her husband Gaylon Umbarger. *Copper and Other Precious Metals* is her first book of poetry, representing the fulfillment of a long-cherished dream. Read more of Elaine's writing at www.elainemcmilian.net or www.elainemcmilian.substack.com.